WHY THE WOMAN IS SINGING ON THE CORNER

A Verse Narrative

Dolores Kendrick

Peter E. Randall Publisher
Portsmouth, New Hampshire
2001

First Edition   1 2 3 4 5 6 7 8 9 10

            Library of Congress Cataloging-in-Publication Data
Kendrick, Dolores, 1927-
    Why the woman is singing on the corner : a verse narrative /
Dolores Kendrick.--1st ed,
    p. cm.
    ISBN 1-931807-00-0
    1. Homeless women--Poetry. I. Title.
    PS3561.E423 W47 2001
    811'.54--dc21

PS
3561
E423
W47
2001
                                               2001048506

Peter E. Randall Publisher
Box 4726, Portsmouth, NH 03802

Distributed by University Press of New England
          Hanover and London

Cover Art: *The White Dress*, silkscreen print by Gwendolyn Knight
Lawrence. (photo courtesy of Workshop Inc., Washington, D.C.)

The poem, "The Stairwell," first appeared in *Through the Ceiling*,
Paul Breman Ltd. Publisher, London, England, 1975

"My Heart Beats for You" written by Josephine Merriweather
Kendrick, Al Fisher and Shep Allen, was originally recorded by
Earl Hines and Billy Eckstein for RCA/Bluebird Records.

Excerpts from this work were published in *Compass Rose*: Vol. 2
No. 1 and Vol. 4 No. 1.

ACKNOWLEDGEMENTS

I wish to thank Mother Mary Thomas OSB, and the
Community of Benedictine Nuns of the Abbey of Saint
Walburga in Colorado, who gave me the peace, time,
and space in which to develop these poems. I also wish
to thank the following people who encouraged, assisted,
and helped to sustain and/or produce this work: John
Kane, Pat Parnell, John Maier, James Landis, Lou Stovall,
the late Rose Lane, Tad Nishimura, the D.C.
Commission on the Arts and Humanities, Mary Frances
Dagostino, Gwendolyn Knight Lawrence, E. Ethelbert
Miller, Grace Cavalieri, Deidre Randall, Peter Randall,
Grace Peirce, Bob and Nadine Thompson, Judy Schultz,
Vivian and Harold Brown and the late Gwendolyn
Brooks, who taught me how to "civilize a space/in which
to play your violin with grace." Finally, to Karen Haith, a
former student, who upon visiting me while I was writ-
ing this book remarked, "Ms. Kendrick, most of us are
just five minutes away from that."

I celebrate you all.

With love always for my brother, Bob.
And for my mother and father, gone to God.

For my days vanish like smoke,
and my bones burn like fire.

Withered and dried up like grass is my
heart ; I forget to eat my bread.
because of my insistent sighing I am
reduced to skin and bone.

I am like a desert owl: I have
become like an owl among the ruins.

Psalm 101. 4-7

The Crazy Woman

I shall not sing a May song.
A May song should be gay.
I'll wait until November
And sing a song of gray.

I'll wait until November.
That is the time for me.
I'll go out in the frosty dark
And sing most terribly.

And all the little people
Will stare at me and say,
"That is the Crazy Woman
Who would not sing in May."

-Gwendolyn Brooks
The Bean Eaters

In memory of
my sister,
Juanita Olga Williams

WitWoman, griot, daughter of laughter and pain,
gift of God.

Sir, give me this water that I may not thirst
or come here to draw.

Samaritan Woman
John 4:16-18

And now she looked ahead.
Something touched her, something moved,
almost violently, toward her vision.
Be still, she thought.
And then she spoke aloud,
"Be still."

WHY THE WOMAN IS SINGING ON THE CORNER

Dialogues: Meddling

Where are you now, old lady?

Garrah is meddling.

"I'm here with you," Phelia speaks slightly. We two make a pair, don't we? Where did you go, Garrah, after you left here? Everybody misses you so. Including me. Never thought I would. We ain't the best of sisters. I don't think I ever knew you, Garrah. All that fighting, all that separating, all that misery. For what, Garrah? For what?

Phelia spits at the sun.
It hurts her eyes.

I know where you are,
but you never did
figure out my little spot
on our ground,
our inheritance.

>   *Garrah is speaking,*
>   *Phelia can't stop her.*

You always believed in demons,
Phelia and you taught me
to be one. Didn't you?
Now, didn't you? Be truthful.
Be honest.

Get you gone, Demon !
And you meant it for me,
your only sister, flesh and blood
of the mother who brought us
to that holy time of re-creation
and taught us to sit down together
and sing.

Here, now sit by me and eat something,
while there's a little silence in the house
and only the floors creak
to tell you the time of day.

Never did like clocks.

"I see you, you know." Phelia is uncomfortable. She shifts in her chair. Her life is uncomfortable. It pains a little, and she doesn't believe too much in medications.

I see you every day of my life

"When you come down those stairs, I go to the kitchen—"

> *To make my coffee*

"—to give you sustenance. You must need it where you are, where you come from..."

> *with a little cream...*

"...not much, just manage to brown it a little..."

> *...hot...*

"...always hot..."

> *...burning the tongue a little...*

"... the stuff that gives you heart attacks when it's that strong..."

> *... that short cup of coffee between the two of us...*

"...then you're gone..."

...No, never gone...
    Out of my eyes I cry to you, Oh, Lord...

"...Garrah, be still.
Tomorrow."

I love you, Garrah.

I remember you in that wheelchair, slightly
tilted, looking for your little paper book that
you had lost from your pocket. I love you,
Garrah. Taking the time to raise me when
Momma died, taking yourself to work in white
folks' kitchens so that I'd never have to. I love
you, Garrah.

My sorrow loves you, and my fear. My little
spindly dreams love you, the way you should
be loved, like summer sky, like last night's rain,
like all those days you never gave to yourself,
like sweet evenings smelling of smiles.

I love you, Garrah.

Not because you gave. That was flesh. That was
natural. But because you *were,* because such a
long time you let me unlove you.

What about tomorrow, Ophelia?

"Come for me."

Not without your shoes on.

"That's right. Bring that laughter with you.
Pale the Prince."

Pale the Prince ! It's late. Go to bed, Old Woman.

"You're older than me. Always was."

Always will be.

Maybe So... Maybe Not

Phelia sputters song.

But it was all a mistake.

Garrah, dead?
No, never.
She was next door
in her own little house
sitting beside Beans,
her cat, making faces at him,
drafting him for her solitudes.

Phelia made it all up.
She liked to tell stories on herself,
she liked the luck of a lie, even
the spread of it around her mouth,
the taste of it when she was hungry.

Besides, she needed a ghost.

The morning was cool
and the birds had taken up
their journeys
and she was alone
and the song was still
except in the frying potatoes,
and the teakettle,
and the sound of water.

Nothing is necessary, she thought.
Not even the praise of love.

There's too much of a day

She thought.

I must find the last light,
she thought.

My kitchen needs cleaning,
she thought.

I'm old. No, I'm not,
she thought.

My house needs dusting,
she thought.

My face needs washing,
she thought.

My hair needs combing,
she thought.

My dreams need a dream,
she thought.

Suddenly, it was tomorrow
and dark,

and the man she lived with
would be home

out of the dark, out of tomorrow.
He would come to her careful waiting,

stretch his arms to the last of her lives,
and make truth of the lie.

How many times would he die for her?
Sometimes she liked to sit and count.

Because he died only for himself,
because she was himself,
and his deaths counted her in.

Inward.

She thought of Garrah,
and she wept.

I'm not an old woman.

Got corns on my toes, a few bunions,
but sweet young women have that. My
life gets across to me, even if it don't
to nobody else. Even if my legs are
wiggly and my arms don't hold things
tight no more. He likes me that way, he
says. But when was the last time I
heard him speak? I mean without a
warning in his voice, without me
listening with a humming in my head.

Without my life hollering and screaming
down my belly even as I give him
my softest smiles and purest pain. Oh,
how it gets across to me: that kind
of love that wants redemption in a man's
body, or even in his words that say,
"come here" and "don't go" and
"don't leave me" and "you'll stay"
and "here, a gift", and gentle gestures
of satin and perfume, that sweeten you
up for a night on the town.

He's the fourth one for that.
I'm just learning to count
with my eyes.

Pale the Prince !

Garrah is prowling

through her dreams again.
I met a man yesterday, Garrah says.
He called your name.

They always call my name, she says.
But this man was a stranger, Garrah smiles.
They are all strange, she whispers,
out of the dark.

No. He came with life, and gave me
an onion to eat because I am
out of the dead.

You are strange, Garrah. Stop singing
like that. You talk in songs that
I can't remember, she says.

Here. For you, Garrah sings.
Take the onion and eat. Soon he will
meet you at the well.

Phelia awoke. No one was beside her.
No strong suggestion of his presence
pressed upon the sheets.

He hadn't come home yet.

A bad dream, she thought.
This one will take centuries.

Strange.
She was always rather strange.
She knew it and loved it.
Sometimes she thought people coveted her strange-
ness,
her manners, her opinions, her laughter,
even her afterthoughts.
People wearied her.
I'm dying, She'd think.
Do they want that, too?
They can have it !
I'll just take myself to Suppie's.
He serves good molasses cake.
(He should, I gave him the recipe !)
Sit there for awhile, make my peace with Him.

They sit on the stoop and talk.

There are so many things
I want to tell you, Garrah,

the way things go, the walk
of every little memory
going down the street before me,

you know, like the backs
of people steadying themselves
before their feet catch in cracks

of concrete when the wind blows
against them. You, Garrah, so tall
and high above.

My memories are all I have.

Garrah listens.

Stop dreaming about me dead,
Ophelia. I ain't dead.
Go about your business

like the woman you are, don't be led
by no dream, no nightmare either.
I'm here, beside you. I'm Garrah,

your sister, late and never.
You're escaping. You don't know
the rules or maybe you've never tried them.

Be good to yourself, ever good.
Nobody's going to do it for you.
Take my hand, now.

Hold onto it.

Phelia hesitates.

Beans jumps in his sleep.

Garrah gets up,
leaves the stoop,
opens the screen-door,
vanishes.

Phelia sits with the palm of one hand open,
her empty grasp lingers in the autumn breeze,
disembodied, breathing.

She remembers her mother's stories about Jo,

her ancestor, a slave woman, who refused to leave
the plantation and follow her husband
in his escape from that life, but kept close
to what she knew, what she had earned, while blessing
his departing footsteps. Jo survived ninety-three years,
died a goat-looking woman, kept the hell of her life
in her apron pocket and dared it to burn or touch her
flesh.

And she never saw her husband again,
and she never kept the lamp burning,
and she never forgot how she loved him,
and she never raised her children
to remember anything but a good father,
for that he was to the day he left.

Now Phelia smiles as she indulges
the strange memory, and the smile
is not exact ; it does not ask much
of her. It merely pauses, casts a silken shadow
passes.

She prays to Jo: you had the best,
that kind of abandonment,
it left you whole. Mine is different.
He never left. His abandonment is to stay,
and sometime tonight, he'll come home,
to this house,
our only kinship,
and select something else to take to the pawnbroker
to keep us going. Oh, if only we both could leave
the plantation and really keep going !

But why should I worry?
He ain't mine anyhow,
just someone I borrowed.
He never wifed me.

In this she abandons her prayer,
in this she finds abandonment safe,
in this Jo's blood quickens in her memory,
bites a little, causing a shivering,
a need to go for a walk
outside the impatient, brooding house, away from her
summoned ancestor who, she knows,
no longer listens,
but waits by the well.

Pieces of the Past

She remembers Billy Eckstein and his song:

walks across the neat living-room,
takes the record from its pouch,
plays it.

Something in your eyes
tells me you're from paradise,
you're an angel in disguise,
my heart beats for you.

Dream beneath the blue,
every dream's a dream of you,
darling, come to me, please do,
my heart beats for you.

Every nightingale seems to sing a lullabye
while a million stars softly twinkle in the sky.

I adore you so
and I'll never let you go,
you were meant for me, I know,
my heart beats for you.

Slowly, ever so slowly
the words drift into the room
like cobwebs and fill it
with shapes and shadows
that filter sunlight and give
a silence to unprotected memory.

Things are soft and gentle,
shimmering for a moment,
then gone.

Lady, you had furs and satins

and a younger body,
and you sat at Art's counter,
graced his Georgia Avenue cafe
or supervised things, whatever would show
you off in suspended animation,
whatever would give him the proper pause
to feel like the man he hoped he was,
passing out cigars,
giving free ice-cream to children,
now and then a beer to his cronies.
And the white tablecloths and napkins beside
the silverplate on the whole round tables,
all the dicktees, the high-fulutin colored couples, com-
    ing to call ;
the women in their silks and velvets,
the men in their pinstripes and gabardines,
a certain royalty in the slow step
of their oblivion. Art's was famous
for the chicken salad, and
the turn-of-the-century bar,
brass and high-toned oak, shipped piece
by muscled piece from San Francisco.
And the waiters, bow-tied, white-aproned,
their steps light and accommodating,
their high handsome faces mellow,
bright, calling forth a rotogravure
of those patrician Negroes that Art had hung
on the cafe's brocade walls
in one of his sepia moods.
Outside, Georgia Avenue danced by
in a slow drag.

And then, all the gambling,
the longing for that slippery power
that seemed to have a price-tag
that he was never able to pay.

No man of us ever is.

Something interrupts her thinking.
Did she hear a siren?
Is there an ambulance out there somewhere?
Who's dying?

Nothing. Nothing.
Just nerves, she repeats over
and over to herself,
and pushes her mind backward once again.

The trouble is they can't read that price-tag
until they're old and blind,
and the braille between them and their dreams
don't work no more, though they know
the signals and speak the language
long before the blind blood congeals
in their eye sockets and puts them to sleep.

No man born of a woman can ever reveal that.

Jo's husband:

Wonder whatever became of him?

You've had three: stolen, run-away, dead.

Did you marry them all at once,
Just in case?
Did you, Phelia?

Want to get gack to Garrah

hear her calling,
asking me about that dollar
I took from her purse yesterday
for the bus.
Asking me to put it back,
though she can't spend it.
Too old, too woman, too dangerous
to herself, that dollar.
That's why I took it,
it was for her salvation.

I guess I've seen the last of money.

Stolen, run away, dead.

One followed another woman
    into the cold of the cradle ;

then he who disappeared without a word
    in the middle of their wedding night ;

but the dead one she loved and loved
    and loved, and that is why he died.

Sometimes, she thought they were all
    the same man.

Psalms

The pavement bears grass,
    I look at it and stumble,

then weep, then stop, and give the grass
    my blessing, and ask the rain to come.

In the noon, the kreelybird cries.
    I don't know its real name,

but it speaks to me in my dead daughter's
    voice.

The power and the glory make noises by my door:
    I open it, and find a withered leaf singing.

But there are no wells in the city:
    there are no wells.

Water comes from rivers and reservoirs
    touched by walls that wells resist.

In the ground are funerals.

I wash myself by the waters of Babylon,
  in my soiled existence, I rinse my fevers

with gauze and ghosts, and manage nothing else:
  that is my prayer.

In the distance are nightcalls hovering over my
  hungers, urging the last light to drift
  unnoticed,

fastening stars to crumbling corners,
  grasping groans of frightened flesh.

I dress a bed in my mind,
  I ask of the room a favor,

I take a day at a time, prepare a meal for the table,
  forget to ask a blessing.

By my bedtable is one Hallelujah,
    One more left, the others are spent.

Will he take it or lose it on a bad bet?
    Make a sales pitch, or will he put it by?

God Almighty, I wonder.

I will rise up, Lord, to join the unmocked,
    the lowly Motherhood stolen from me
    so long ago.

My heart has betrayed me, it gives me phantoms ;
    my head has loved me, it gives me arguments
    of hope.

Which will I trust?

I hear sounds where nothing lives,
    I hear birds where none sing,

I smell promises in swelling dung heaps,
  I take what I can when I can get it.

Yet, one who is alive in death waits upon me,
  Your ghost is yet to be born, Garrah,

and I'm speaking to it !

Stolen, Run-Away, Dead

A man came in

and asked for water,
she served him,
he drank slowly, deliberately,
and watched her borrowed face,
then he left.
And all the while
she seemed given to him
in some strange way.
On the counter
was a large tip
and the glass that held
the water stood brightly
touched by a song of sun.
He knows me, she thought.
From somewhere he knows me,
and she moved her aching fingers
over her withering brown hands.

Horizons are in her mind.
She hears a voice:
this is the place to draw water
if you are thirsty. I am.
Announce me.
But you have no bucket, she says.
You have. That's all I need.
And what am I to do? she asks aloud.
Give me your misery. Forget mine.

His voice becomes Tolly Boggs,
who is sitting on a stool
at the bar, staring at her
and wanting a beer.

What's your misery, Tolly? she says.
My wife ain't home, he smiles,
and it's time for my libation.
I need some oilin'.

The place is empty, now.
And the white tablecloths have
long since disappeared.
Customers, when they come,
eat on bare tables with paper napkins,
and the food is short-order.
The walled brocade is ripped and rotting,
and the bar stools complain under pressure.
The brass and wood no longer glisten,
but an occasional smudge of sunlight
reveals a listening past, somewhat
more distant than San Francisco.

She gives Tolly his beer,
takes the money, rings it up, laughs,
and says, *the greens are good today,*
goes to the kitchen to stir the pot,
Suddenly, she sings.

She wants to find Jo,
listen to Garrah,
give living things her life,
and her wish speaks back to her:
find the well, fetch,
draw, the water can accommodate you.
What is soft, reasonable, knowing
is yours, what cleans as it escapes.
It is what you do best,
it is what the earth does best,
and even that will not make you holy.

Art would come in the night

take her, sleep on her breast,
what he would not take,
she would give.
The wife in her had long since drowned
and he had found the body.
I don't want no man to own me anymore,
she calls to herself. Alone, she finds
her shivering voice a companion.
Better this way, he can leave,
and I can leave, and we don't need
no partin' papers, and she washes
the last customer's dish,
closes the restaurant's door,
goes out to look for him,
a word or two slipping from her lips.

And the three lost husbands.
They left one way or another.
But she had only one child,
the one whose hand she held in the darkness
while she was asleep, that one she lullabied to sleep,
that one she spoke to when the rooms were
about to kill her, that one she created the three lies for,
that one she took to parties over at Suppie's and later
at Dolly-Rose's fashion show that always showed off
the prettiest of colored women. That one she had while
she was defying nature.

She thought of her lost life.
That child, that child, that haunted child.

Now I tell you child, we Black women must be careful.
Not too much out here for us, you know?
Give me your hand.
There.
We're bound together you and me.
Mother and daughter.
Sometimes I believe I came out of the sea, the big ocean
while the waves were yelping and the sky screaming and
I gave me a birth. You know, from water.
Wasn't no man involved. Didn't need one. Only me
and that yelping sea, bringing forth from an opening in
the sky in pain.
You see child, we Black women must be careful because
I think sometimes we defy nature, and when we do that
we have to be punished.

She shivers.

What happened to those hungry men?

One followed another woman into the cradle:

(Instead in her passing.
she finds Buster and blinks
her eyes in recognition.)

His ties were always right,
and he laughed when he was in trouble.
She married him on a whim that failed.
His manliness was strong enough
to hold her but not himself,
and when he stumbled, he brought her roses.
The last bunch was billed to the other woman,
who danced upon needles and made hungry jokes
about it so that he could join himself
with easy come-and-go.
Her fragile talent didn't reach that far,
and Buster had a yearning for women
who knew the right steps.

They made good teachers.

Then he who disappeared without a word
in the middle of their wedding night:

Oh, Sakson !

So fine and tender !

    long in heart,

        legs like sylphs

going places before sundown.

      She married his sweet hopes

         that were too delicate

            to include her,

     she needed inclusions

        her arm in his

        the soft hold of promises

    that he designed

        like the outfits she wore ;

        the business clothes he kept

to impress friends he sought.

He was successful

(right down her alley!)

The doubts she carried

into a sickness of expediency,

for marriage to such a man

was just that. She knew. She knew.

Even as she turned from him

that secret night

she heard him howling in his smile.

Then he was gone.

But the dead one she loved and loved
and loved and that is why he died.

She buried him before the sun made myths,
of her deliverance.

Why is death so ordinary,
so available? A woman has rights.
Loving is one of them.
He told her that she smothered him:
the woman won't let me breathe, he said,
the rooms listened, and all the murmuring monsters
locked behind doors in the shadows of their dreams:
Baby, you squeeze too tight, hug too hungry,
he said, a man's gotta bum out now and then.
He found a sickness.
He could not tolerate the attack of her heart upon his.
She buried him before the sun made him a liar.
He did not complain.

Good colored woman.

Disappearances

Back in her house

without Art, she remembered her childhood,
the mother who had left her and Garrah
at The Shelter, a holding place.
Once she came for them,
tried to steal them through the iron fence
that was designed to make her invisible,
the hand reaching out,
*too late, **Mama**,* Phelia screams in the dark,
Her memory rattles: there is no hold, nothing.

That was the last time she saw her mother.

There was the stairwell:
holidays when mothers came to visit,
and see and watch and hug and leave again.
Garrah often walked the stairwell to wait,
if only for a shadow, but she, Phelia, knew better.

Sometimes the stairwell, in her mother's voice,
spoke to her.

I will give you a stairway,
wind it to fit the dance
in your eye and leave but you
to climb the circle you embrace as me.

While the bartered children sang,
That's my momma ! That's my momma !

And she spoke back,

That's my

   Merry Mother,

Mother-gone, you won't come
ever to Christmas. What is

   Christmas?

Dance Mother ! Dance !

Stables of the dance squat in her memory, cold and
damp. Christmas without. The stairwell listening,
creaking, bellowing with good Mothers dancing
Darling, embracing their lost. Tears. No sleep. Unmade
beds. The holiday for visiting mothers in a home for
abandoned children. Crumbling Christmas snow touches
a crib of her hope, this child whose mother never
comes for Christmas.

No room at the inn. Bear her somewhere else. Bear her
to a little gut of emptiness. No kings. No star. No
lambs or shepherds. Not even a play of flight. Only
the thin stairway circling, screaming, the skin
of its arms dry and loose. Merry night Merry child
Merry woman reaching through a locked gate (once
upon a time) to open small hands.
What is Christmas?

And she made her own commandment:

I will not come to the Stairwell again.
There is no dance upon it.
The stairway is but straw
and Christmas comes upon it
like a scythe.

Then the aunt she had never seen,
finding her in a park, selling flowers
from baskets she had woven
in a strange act of survival.

That was long ago in Rhode Island, she murmurs
        aloud.
Remember, Garrah, we left together.
We wept.
Aunt Tillie told us to be brave,
somebody was waiting to take us in,
cure our abandonment.
(It's a disease, isn't it?)

We didn't need no mother.

What about Papa?
Working on the railroad all his life,
chef for all the WhiteRich
in those days when WhiteRichRailroad
came together like WhiteMan'sBurden.
Oh, how they loved his burden meals !

Phelia remembering with grits of her jaw
straining at its muscle, poised
to answer questions she should not ask,
his half-done chicken on the table,
chef that he was, a dying thing to see,
his not knowing, she not understanding that which
more deeply than the half life that
now represented him and his dumbness to what he had
    sired:
his coming home to die, and I buried him, Garrah,
because you didn't like his voice,
even in death, that voice that was
so silent when we went to the Shelter.
Where was he, Garrah? Why did Papa give Momma
that right? Who did I really bury?
Much of me, I guess,
and too much of Momma.

She wants to conjure up Garrah again,
who sits by her kitchen window,
peeling potatoes.

She hums

as she washes the dishes.
Art sits at the cash-register,
counting receipts.

There is a balm in Gilead

Now and then a word washes out.

To make the wounded whole

Art looks up curiously.
She's never sung Spirituals before,
She ain't the "Negro Spiritual" type.

There is a balm in Gilead

Her voice rises,
he checks out the money
one last time,

To cure the sin-sick soul!

pockets it, comes to her,
catches her shoulder,
whispers through the words,
I'm your balm,
smiles,
goin' out to get you some gladiolus,
wait up for me,
kisses her on her breast,
watches it sink,
leaves.

She looks over the pit
left by his absence
and wonders if Jo sang
that pretty song, too,
or if those struggling slaves
had another way to keep
the demons at bay,

and she touches with her eyes
something unseeable:
Garrah's by me *somewhere*
but she's just good for teasin'.

Phelia wants to go
to the well, but she doesn't know
where to find it.
(What is there about water
that cleanses first
then washes?)

The ache of too many leavings
and forgettings has dried dreams
like the walls of her womb,
she wants the healing waters
that those church people

talk about
to wash off the sores
of women like herself,
she wants something
of a groundswell.

There must be a well in Gilead.

Garrah is about to die

and keep her promise:
to go softly, silently,
no pain, in her sleep,
she just moves on.

Her funeral is within the week.
Where is tomorrow?
Phelia thinks: she will
cremate her, as Garrah wanted,
back to earth.

Spread me in your garden,
Ophelia, let me give you
purely, what God can touch
with His feet, walk upon in roses,
weep in wildflowers,
then you will not grieve.

So Garrah said,
So Phelia makes into song,
So her litany begins.

Garrah lives ! she thinks.
and then, *Announce Him* !

Phelia remembers

Garrah can't desert her flesh,
I thank her for that
in my deepest passion.

Pale the Prince !
That secret litany
only we can speak
in tongues.

Oh, (she smiles comfortably
within herself) that's just
a family Hallelujah !
Garrah and me
holdin' on.

Phelia buries part of the ashes
in the garden by her bedroom
window, something she had nursed
and tended like her loves:

the nasturtium, snap dragon,
woodlily, rose, hyacinth,
sunflower, daffodil, tulip,
the lives of her delivery.

(Later, she would sit for long hours and eat her garden
in separate flowers, one by one, and she would feel her
madness coming on like a thunderstorm meddling its
way through the smallest bud, or the tenderest root.)

And with a tablespoon she lifts what's left
of Garrah's grain bit by smiling bit
into a small tin box,
locks it, and threads it through
with a thin purple ribbon,
to tie around her neck.

Then she goes to the old field
long into Virginia
where slave folk live in unmarked graves,
and looks for Jo,

whom she knows
is nowhere in that place.

You have a child

she dies
    and you don't know why.

    There is a night
        that comes for one reason

        and one only:

        the child.

That night
    is from Hell.
        You know, you've seen it.

You saw it
    come in clusters
        cradle Lolly to its bosom

ask her
    for a kiss, and she gave it,
        though she cried and shook
and ran from
    the blanket that covered her
        into a dark corner

where she
    thought it was light,
        her eyes open and shut

and shut and open,
    the phantom sleep
        cursing her all the while.

Demon dreams
    curdled in her cries
        and you couldn't wake her,

or touch her
    or the shock would kill her,
        so you sat in the dark corner

beside her
    holding her while she sweated
        and moaned, and you could hold only

her wet body
    shivering like she had eaten
        her shadow, over and over again.

What did she see?
    Me trying to seal her pain? (she says aloud
    deaf to her own voice) or maybe she was me as
    I was born

my life in hers forgiven
    and I am seeing now
    what absolves and resurrects.

Her voice runs away. She tries to capture it again.
    But it has buckled within her.
    Tucked itself within
    the crowds of her inner self
    that now speak once more.

Yet, you know
    one day she will not wake from all that,
    and the day comes.

You touch her,
    and she has gone cold
    you can almost see the frost on her face.

And your heart sinks,
    and your skin withers
    and you become old.

Tiny demons live in dust, your daughter's coldness
says. I know the feel of it, you say.

And all the rest

gone, not knowing of your careful promises
loosed within your skin, darkening,
wrinkling, staining, dissolving,
changing all the appearances.

Just a little of 'lookin' good' left:

to cure the sin-sick soul !

It is a crisp, November day:

the sky, the trees, the leaves
obey it. There is an eloquence
in Phelia's voice as she places
a small portion of Garrah's ashes
into the second ground.

She murmurs disconnected old things
to sounds that are distorted
and strangely tuned.

It is her music.

This time there is poetry praying
for her. This time there is
no sound of Garrah in her head,
other than a scratch of drifting leaves,
small winds easing over spare
limbs of oak and elm, mute colors pausing in
poems of safety, solitude, submission,
order, grace forming a pattern
of song in her mind.

Phelia chants quietly, under her breath

She kneels to ground,
touches the flesh
of her ancestors
with the tips of her fingers,
hands roaming over blackened dirt
that now is the body
of their bold ascensions.

She kisses graves, unmarked
in the burial sun,
the sleep of their dreams
startles her, then quiets.

She knows their presence,
after all that was the voice
of Garrah, the continuity
of bloodline that would
someday remember and forgive all.

And she now in the cold
and straggly wind, where colors
fade into deep and other
beauty, sometimes merging
to make a mystery of
the familiar, would recite
her secret litany

(which Garrah had taught her):

for small things lost,
          pale the prince !

for large things kept,
          pale the prince !

for the disguises of love,
          pale the prince !

for nothing bound,
          pale the prince !

And the prince
who is the messenger
of nightmares,
who begets pain
come as privilege,
pales, disappears.

Colors now are rushing by her eyes,
in risky rainbows like dusky
imitations longed for by her
heart.

She would carry the poem
inside her, like the woman
who had the holy conception:
Little gifts were enough.

It was all she wanted.

Take the prayer, Garrah,
she thinks as she rises
from the ground.

I'll talk with you day and night,
can't help it, because you stayed.

You kept the faith.

That way, nobody leaves,
not even Momma.
When the poem comes,
and the water breaks,
I'll settle down
and go to sleep.

I think I'll go, now, Garrah,
Art may be waiting,
Gotta get his dinner, you know.

Tomorrow is Sunday,
Is it?
Can't remember.
But I'm on my way to church,
I guess. Tomorrow.

Must purify myself to announce Him.

At the Well

On Sunday she takes the water.

It does not rush or suffocate,
it runs softly through her forty-eight years,

leaving them wet within her,
intact. The poverty of pain unbidden recedes
with ghost-like rhythms into the dark.

The minister says the words,
but she finds the lyric.

The well is opened,
she hears its clean echoes as she imagines
herself drawing water, as her thirst is satisfied,
cleansed.

She rises from the water's brisk embrace,
her eyes shut, dripping sunlight struggling
through brittle windows.

She feels the minister's calloused hand
on her shivering shoulder, and nods
an unspoken self-litany.

Her mind drifts:

I go to the well and draw water,
and wait and hope there's a little
of that dryness that gathers
in my throat that will go away
if I can manage to get me
a long, cool drink. Sometimes the water
is clear, sometimes it ain't, things floating around in it,
and sometimes I know the well ain't real,
it aint' really there, you know,
ain't no well ain't no bucket,
and there ain't no water,
not the kind I need, the kind
that takes the dryness
out of my soul
washes from the inside,
flushes out all the emptiness
and shame and dying things,
lets me feel a small bit pure,
just that, gives me myself back again
like a newborn babe, all soft and pretty,
and clear-eyed, lets me know that
in this precious birth I am not alone,
nothing deserts, nothing takes, nothing leaves,
nothing falls away, no scales or sores
or scabs or scars that let you know
a killing has taken place.

Dolores Kendrick   73

Met a man once,
reminded me of the man in the cafe.
He spoke to me in a maze of words.
I thought he was a prophet
because he had my number.
That's all I remember.

Except
I keep going to that Phantom well,
and Jo, she ain't there,
never was, never will be,
but I'm there
watching, thinking, grieving, singing,
swallowing my life with the water.

I'll prayer me a well one day.

She goes back to her house

her baptism in her blood,
and murmurs things to herself,
things she mustn't forget.

Where is Art?
She saw him last night,
or was it in the morning?

Or was it a week ago?
a month? There's a stinging hum
in the last of her moans,
in something jumbled in her dream:

the baptism, the well,
which is the dream?
Which did she know?

She mothers her kitchen.
It resists.
Where is the teakettle,
the tea-cup, the lumps of sugar?

Where are things?
She always knew how to put everything
carefully in the right places.

What happened to the cornbread?
And the honey?

Phelia is beside herself

As she dances through her rooms.
In her mellow footsteps
she hears her echo.

I will dress for the occasion.

Something borrowed, something blue,
my fine silk stockings, the last pair,
the silk scarf around my hair,
paisley-red, that's the best,
the yellow earrings,
sets off the arriving gray:
(she giggles to herself)
complements my laughing white dress.

Get those toe nails,
they've gotten long and angry again.

Arri——i—i——i—iv—ing gray !
Yes !
Amen !

Now where's that perfume Art gave me?
Had it on the dresser,
what happened to that perfume !
Art stole it from me,
gave it to his new woman.

Art, you stole my perfume !
Art, you stole my sweet gray !

(She takes a scream blooming in her breast,
and chokes it back, but it pushes through
her lungs, leaving her exhausted.)

Art ! You thief !
You stole my sweet gray !

Things never break where they fall:

she is beginning to love the years of her Self.

Gray perfume.

Art give it to me.
Gotta find it !

She forgets,

goes to her closet,
finds an old fur-piece,
something falsely animal,
to wrap around her shoulders.

It's cold out there,
it's very cold out there,
she thinks.

Bring me the sun, Art.
Come with it between your lips,
and I'll kiss it
and get warm,
she says aloud.

Find the perfume, woman,
she hears his voice somewhere out of her reach.

She looks into her hands,
sees her reflection in them,

Gasps.

The perfume no longer matters.
It has a sour smell anyway:
her nostrils no longer know the difference.

For a moment
things are confused:
the perfume, her unnoticeable gray hairs,
what seals, what confines,
what chokes,
what sings, what blesses,
what announces.

Matters are only matters,
she hears in her head,
for her long thinking is finished
and only the bones are left.

Dolores Kendrick   79

I have a Mission,

she thinks.
I am not alone.
Never again !
I've been given a large tip
for a small service,

and I ain't going to squander it.

Look at me, Garrah.
Do I look alright?
Going to announce Him,
like He told me,
maybe something's waiting
for me there,
where I go.

Maybe He's there
waiting for another glass
of Phelia's cold water.

She powders her face,
dresses her lips with
layers of lipstick,
blushes her cheeks a rich red.

One heel of her shoe
slightly run-over,
she goes downstairs,
brushes her lips with her forefinger
and scrawls across
the kitchen table:

Art, I'm gone !

She does not remember
his last note to her.

Rise, Sally, Rise !

On a bright August morning

she sees the man again.
He is smiling.
He has not deserted her, she thinks.
He is there before her,
sometimes beside her,
wishing her little triumphs,
impelling a strength,
unleashing tides of recovery
within her. She knows Him now.

He comes from her past,
but He can't get by,
too much death in the way.
She must open the gate,
let Him in,
before He melts before
her very eyes.

Yet, she knows His existence,
His Being. His presence
cannot stride itself without
her introduction. He is her
quest. So chosen, she is no longer left alone.

14th Street

has an ache in its belly.
Traffic is agitated,
pavements are hot,
the D.C. street steams
in summer sounds.
Above, a choirloft of birds
comment upon the sages of the air:
pigeons practicing polevaults
under plane-driven sky.

People make choices:
a cab, the bus or Metro,
and whisper their complaints
into the ear of a listening cloud.

The cacophony pleases Phelia ;
long ago 14th Street
was an avenue, wide and graceful,
a trolley-car track ribboning
its long and graceful limb
moving from uptown to the U Street
corridor where people came
to pay homage to a Blues
and Jazz courtship:
Ella, Chick Webb, Dizzy Gillespie,
Cab Calloway, Billy Eckstein,
Billie Holiday, the divine Sarah,
Louis Armstrong. From U Street the limb
creaked to the narrows of Downtown,

carrying a slight hum, and that was all.
Now the trees in aging
speak stories about themselves,
converse with the street
gone old and slightly bony,
no longer plump and full of honey,
a debris in its voice.

The city corner

is hot. The summer breeze
is slow and teasing, but Phelia
hardly notices.

She clenches her fur around
her neck (because she no longer
accepts the seasons).

This is her cold, her winter
of frugal comforts. She prefers
to enjoy it.

Her stockings have slipped,
one almost down to her ankle:
the little things.

She pinches a few ashes
from Garrah's box and sifts
them to the breeze.

People stare.

Garrah is never far away,
she murmers,
and that is my keeping, my blessing
on this world.

Between the sprinkles of ashes,
she calls out not Garrah's name,
but His:

I announce Him !
I announce Him !

and she turns and looks Him
in the eye.

She is outside herself,
watching herself walk
to the corner backwards.
Oh, doesn't she look pretty !

Her heart beats wildly.
She hears it dance within her,
she sees Jo keeping step,
not herself, but Jo.

As she releases her words
into the supple air, roaming children
touch her body, whirl her around
until she is dizzy and the street-corner
becomes a complex of illusions.

The children sing as they
turn her about:

Little Sally Walker
sitting in a saucer,
rise, Sally, rise,
wipe your dirty eyes,
put your hands on your hip
and let your backbone slip.

Hey ! shake it to the East,
and shake it to the West,

and shake it to the one
that you love the best !

Phelia shivers.
The dizziness engulfs her
with a quivering delight.
She shakes her hips
as the children sing.
She does not notice
their mocking laughter
nor one girl's scamper
for a stone to place
under her feet.

She does not trip.
She docs not fall.
Now she is royal
and song and dance

are her ablutions.

A Coming has been invoked:
nothing less.
She has seen to it.
She is a good provider.

No time for sorrow, woman.

Soon the children scatter
and take their voices with them.

She feels a little pain.
Another absence.

Then she sings again.

It is the widow's song,

the mother's song,
the daughter's song,
the song of the first universe
born out of nothing,
the sisters' song,

the song of stars and winds of the night,
the song of Jo in her cold bed,
the song of fire and flood,
the song of prophecy,
the song of denial and hope,
the song of the next morning
already seeded in the lung.

And it had all begun in her bedroom

one night when she was alone
and talked with spectres and faces
and voices unconnected with any
bodily thing, that time when she saw
her own image reflected not in water
or mirrors, but in flesh and unleashed spirit.

Now the song surges within her,
almost to a scream,
and then grows silent.

There is no death in me,
she thinks, my song
is just resting.

And the people watching and moving away,
some whispering, others calling out,
crazy old Black woman ! as she brings
the meandering melody to her throat
in strains of tones and unremembered words,
hums and hollers and strange behaviors.

She likes the feel of the song.

Heat moves into her eyes.
Her vision bleeds:
whenever she handles it,
she sprinkles Garrah's ashes
into its wounds
and attends its call.

I announce Him ! she sings.

And folds her song between
each dangerous syllable

Someone stops to watch
as she struggles with an illusive note,
but hears the vanished children's voices
in her own.

A piece of her crippled shadow
moves against the earth,
softens it.

A small crowd assembles to which she bows,
graciously.

Everything is complete.

In this she finds family.

Lord, we know what we are

but know not what we may be.

—Ophelia, from William Shakespeare's *Hamlet*

"I read some of the new poems by Dolores Kendrick and they took the dryness out of my soul. Kendrick is the First Lady of Poetry in Washington D.C. Once again she examines the hearts of black women. Kendrick mixes holy water with words. Her poems will bless you. They will make you sing. Go tell it on the corner."
    — E. Ethelbert Miller, Director
      African American Resource Center, Howard University

"*The Women of Plums* established Dolores Kendrick as a major figure in American Letters, giving us new hope for this country's literature. We heard the voices in history that could not be stilled, filling us with the blood of our own humanness. Now we behold a new Kendrick work, *Why the Woman is Singing on the Corner.* Thank you. Thank you for these women, and for going to the deepest well once more. We were so thirsty."
    — Grace Cavalieri, Producer/Host
      "The Poet and the Poem from the Library of
      Congress"

"Dolores Kendrick's new work stuns with its stark power. Read it as a novel. Move into the mind of Ophelia, the singing woman. Eavesdrop on her interior dialogues with the spirit of her sister, Garrah, and the others who people her nightmares. Don't look for another *Women of Plums.* Those slave women sang their stories; Phelia is living—and reliving—hers. Kendrick's story-telling skills have intensified as she spirals with her protagonist into the depths of the dark night of the soul. We don't want to acknowledge the existence of street people, but Kendrick makes us stop and look and understand. She has created a living, breathing woman who, at the end, is able, with the power of her faith, to pull together all the pieces of her life in a song of triumph."
    —Pat Parnell, author of *Snake Woman and Other
      Explorations, Finding the Female in Divinity*

"These poems, each satisfying in itself, gradually and subtly cycle beyond that satisfaction into the absorbing life story of 'The Woman,' which in turn begins to touch on the stories of all women, and of a people. To discover Dolores Kendrick's answer to the title question is to have a deep and poetically powerful reading experience."

—John Kane,
English Department, Phillips Exeter Academy

DATE DUE
